Man. United

Poetry in Motion

AuthorHouse™ UK Ltd.
500 Avebury Boulevard
Central Milton Keynes, MK9 2BE
www.authorhouse.co.uk
Phone: 08001974150

First published by AuthorHouse 6/29/2011

ISBN: 978-1-4567-8422-5 (sc)

This book is printed on acid-free paper.

authorHOUSE®

Man. United

Poetry in Motion

Stan Warburton

Man. United - Poetry in Motion is different to any other Sports History book that you have ever read before.

It is a potted history of Manchester United but all written in rhyme. It is 'unique,' it is 'quirky,' easily readable, fully illustrated and a book that you are able to pick-up, put down and not miss out by doing so.

Author Stan Warburton has been a Manchester United fan ever since his dad first took him as a young boy. Even when his family moved to live in Colwyn Bay with Stan as a twelve year old, he never lost his love or support for the Reds, travelling to Old Trafford as often as he could.

'Poetry in Motion' is the Title poem and tells of some of Man United's greatest matches, the times when they have really been 'on song'.

'Why is it that Poets are mean, when it comes to writing of the football scene,' is the first line of his poem 'My Football Team' which combines Stan's love of Man. United and poetry.

These are just two of thirty widely differing poems about all things Man United.

I am sure you will love reading his first football poetry book.

Illustrations are faded slightly to allow reading of the poems.

Stan......thank you for your poems and I just thought I would drop you a wee line...to say...the poems are excellent and I very much enjoyed reading them, recounting some wonderful memories......
Sir Alex Ferguson CBE.

The author would like to thank and give due acknowledgements for pictures in this book to the following:-

Colorsport.   Manchester Evening News.   Getty Images.   And a special thankyou to Manchester United Football Club for the many pictures taken by the author in and around Old Trafford. Every effort has been made to trace the copyright of other older photographs used and we would like to apologise for any omissions. The author would be pleased to include appropriate acknowledgement in any subsequent book.

Also many thanks to Barry Dean for all his computer work help and to John Coker for his encouragement..

Man United.........Poetry in Motion

Index

Man United.....Poetry in Motion

In a European match in 66,
United played Benfica away.
90,000 people in the crowd,
To watch these great teams play.
Within twelve minutes Best had scored two,
Then helped to set up three more.
Portuguese fans had never before witnessed,
A home game with a 1-5 score.
They had to admit United played football
Of a 'mesmerising' kind,
But when United are on song, it's…
…Poetry in motion, you'll find.

In Wembley, London in 68,
The European Cup Final was played.
Old enemies from the past,
And another good match is made
Its United verses Benfica again,
Which team now will play 'something like?'
'One all' going in to extra time,
Then United start to 'get on their bike.'
In a ten minute spell United score three,
And United have won, it's plain.
They left it late to be on song, but it's…
…Poetry in motion again.

In a Premier League game in 98,
United played Forest away,
At 4--1 up and in control,
Fergie thought he would 'call it a day.'
Brought Yorky off and put Solskjaer on,
'just for the last quarter,'
Ole scored 4 and at 8--1 down,
Forest were lambs to the slaughter.
They said United were brilliant and asked,
"could they use their magic potion?"
It's just Man United on song, Fergie said "it's
…Poetry in Motion."

In September 2001,
United played the 'Spurs' away,
Three nil down at half time,
We knew it was Tottenham's day.
In the second half United came out
And were like a different team.
Scored 5 goals in half an hour,
For fans it was a dream.
They could not believe their difference,
Now playing so sublime.
But when Man United play on song, it's…
…Poetry in Motion Time.

In the quarter final of the Champions League,
Roma won the home leg 2-1,
In the return at Old Trafford, Roma's goal
Was hit by a 'cluster bomb.'
United scored 7, could have been 11,
And Roma completely outplayed.
They did score a consolation goal,
But the inevitable was only delayed.
Roma's players were low, they did not believe,
That they could have done anymore
But when Man United's playing on song, it's…
…Poetry in Motion for sure.

In April in the year 2009,
United played Tottenham at home,
United 2-0 down at half time,
The Spurs fans were singing alone.
Then the second half started, and United
Came out fighting to a man.
They scored 5 goals in a twenty minute spell,
And said "sing now if you can."
Spurs players said, "they've done this before,
We're playing to the wrong notion,"
Because when Man United's on song, it's pure…
…Poetry in Motion.

The Birth of a Legend

In a city in England in Eighteen Seventy Eight,
The start of a story, I would love to relate.
It's the birth of a team who play fantastic football,
But when it all started, its beginnings were small.
A few lads got together in the locomotive sheds,
They said, "lets start a team", hence the birth of the reds.
Newton Heath L &Y Railway, the football teams name,
And so it began, the long road to fame.

Playing in green and yellow, the "Heathens" were born,
And from the beginning took Manchester by storm.
Newton Heath "Loco" went surging ahead,
Got best players around by giving them jobs at the sheds.
In 1885 the Manchester Cup beckoned,
They were finalists in't first year and won it in't second.
In fact they got to the final, the first 8 years out of 9,
You could say the train was running on time.

The way that they played was pure football science,
And in 1891 they joined the Football Alliance.
They beat Ardwick 3-1, which makes a nice little ditty,
Cause Ardwick went on to become Manchester City.
So against the sky blues, good foundations were laid,
We can recant how we beat them, the first time we played.
But not content with the kudos that gave us,
The very next season, we got Football League status.

This step-up in class was a different league to be in,
They played the first seven games without getting a win.
But in their eighth game all doubts were gone,
They played Wolverhampton Wanderers & beat them 10-1
It seems strange that the Heathens very first win,
(such a great score, what a game to be in)
Became their record score, for any league game,
And over 100 years later, it's still exactly the same.

But ten years later, such a different fate:-
The club declared bankrupt, they padlocked the gate.
They needed a saviour, all money was gone,
Club Captain 'Harry Stafford', set out to find one.
He went to a fund raiser, with his St. Bernard dog,
Trying to find a way through this financial fog.
He said, "invest in Newton Heath, it's the way to go",
But it was the St. Bernard that stole the show.

John Henry Davies, a local business man,
Said "I would like to buy that dog if I can".
"I'll have to decline that offer" the club captain said,
"But why not buy the club instead"!
So he bought the set up but said "it can't be the same,
The first thing we'll do is give the club a new name".
With new investment, they all got excited,
And Newton Heath became Manchester United.

As Manchester United, the train steamed on,
All fear of closure now completely gone.
Now they relaxed and played a great game,
And with success, the beginnings of fame.
The train once again was right on time,
Won the League in 1908 and the Cup in 09.
With the club now well run,the board made sure,
They would never again need a financial cure.

And the rest is history, Manchester United became,
The best English club ever to play the game.
United continued, the train still on the line,
Won every possible club trophy since that time.
Great players, great managers, trophies galore,
Manchester United continue to score.
But this world famous team, 'it beggars belief,'
It all began in 'locomotive sheds' of little Newton Heath.

Sir Matt Busby

The war is over, its Nineteen Forty Five,
Normality gradually returns,
Football is awakening, its coming alive,
But the pitch is covered in ferns.
United in tatters, no money, no ground,
They needed a manager, Matt Busby they found.

Young Scotsman, fresh home from the war,
Had played for City and Liverpool,
He had never managed a team before,
But to be sure, he was no mans fool.
He looked at the ground, bombed into rubble,
Smilingly said, "This'll take some time and trouble.

Matt Busby was a man, not known to shirk,
And so to the task he began.
"I've never known anyone to die of hard work,"
Became his master plan.
Didn't have a pitch, but some good players he found,
Had to play all home games at Man City's ground.

He had new ideas for coaching his team,
Wore a track suit for a start.
To sit in an office just wasn't his scene,
Liked to work with his players on the park.
The new methods obviously came to fruition,
Finished Runners Up in his very first season.

With players Carey, Chilton, Crompton, Cockburn too,
Anderson, Morrisey in his team.
Plus Aston, Delaney, Rowley, Pearson, and Mitten for you,
To win a trophy was his dream.
In the F.A. Cup, drew a first division team every round,
All a home draw, but played each on a different ground.

His idea was to play with attacking flair,
Which the fans just flocked to see.
If they scored more than opponents he just didn't care,
And the supporters lapped it up with glee.
They beat Blackpool at Wembley to win his first Cup,
And again in the league they finished Runners Up.

United finished Runners Up four years on the trot,
And then in Nineteen Fifty Two,
They finally finished the season in the top spot,
The rebirth of the reds was true.
Matt Busby the forefather of the modern day United,
A beautiful team and the flame reignited.

Another innovation was his accent on youth,
Realised there was lots of good kids.
Though his first great team was getting 'long in the tooth,'
He didn't need any transfer bids.
Gathered all the good youngsters from far and near,
Coached them to play good football without any fear.

Won the F.A. Youth Cup for it's first five years,
Introduced youth into his team.
Gradually replaced ageing players without any tears,
The 'Busby Babes' became his dream.
These young players became his second great side,
But finished only fifth in Nineteen Fifty Five

Now it was Colman, Edwards, Foulkes and Gregg,
Roger Byrne, Mark Jones, Billy Whelan.
Johnny Berry, Dennis Viollet, Tommy Taylor, David Pegg
These Babes improving all season.
Now playing great football with this youthful mix,
Won the league by eleven points in Nineteen Fifty Six.

Now the European Cup had began the previous year,
Champions Chelsea invited from our land.
The English F.A refused and said 'no team from here,'
But Matt Busby made a resolute stand.
He wanted to match his players against the best,
And by entering Europe, this would be the test.

So Manchester United entered the European Cup,
Pioneers in Europe for England,
Both players and fans just 'lapped it up,'
Beat Anderlect and Borussia Dortmund.
Had no floodlights yet at United's ground,
So home games again at Maine Road, every round.

Had some great victories in Europe that year,
Only beaten in the semi final stage.
Against the mighty Real Madrid they shed a few tears,
But the Busby babes were coming of age.
Lost the F.A. Cup Final with only ten fit men,
Won the league easy, by a 'country mile,' yet again.

After winning the league, they were in Europe once more,
And in February, Nineteen Fifty Eight.
Beat Red Star Belgrade, with aggregate score of 5-4,
Another Semi-Final was a date.
But fate stepped in, ...most would never return,
As on a Munich Airfield, ... the aeroplane burned.

Eight of the babes were taken from that squad,
And two more would never play again.
The life of Matt Busby was in the hand of God,
The 'Sunshine' had turned to 'Rain.'
All his work on the 'fabric' was torn apart at the seam,
Manchester mourned the cruel end, of his great young team.

After recovering from his injuries, Busby started again,
He had a football team to rebuild.
To the disaster survivors he added a few men,
         Like Albert Quixall, Maurice Setters, David Herd.
He also signed Noel Cantwell and then Denis Law,
And with Paddy Crerand he was ready for war.

Already had Billy Foulkes, David Gaskell, Tony Dunne,
And Johnny Giles from across the Irish Sea.
And on the other wing he had Bobby Charlton,
They reached the Cup Final in 1963.
Leicester City were the favourites, in fact, odds on,
With a goal from Law and two from Herd, United won it 3-1.

So Busby's third great team was well on its way,
But really he wanted the league,
To re-enter Europe was the target, he'd say
The European Cup had become his dream.
But in Sixty Three he found a boy, better than the rest.
Came from Northern Ireland and his name was Georgie Best.

Busby fielded two 17 year olds, that day in late sixty three,
Striker Dave Sadler and Winger George Best.
With a victory over West Brom everyone could see,
He now had a team to take on the rest.
Champions the next year, followed by six years of success,
But the European cup was his absolute nemesis.

United back in Europe after nine long years,
Could this be the time that they'd win.
Teams from Helsinki and East Germany held no fears,
With the Reds in the Quarter Final again.
Drawn against Benfica, the mighty Portuguese team,
If they can overcome these then it's on with the dream.

Won an exciting first game, just 3-2 at Old Trafford,
The winning score can't be enough.
Would we ever get this big cup in the cupboard?
To play Benfica away was tough.
But the Stadium of Light 'wowed' to the football of Best,
He scored two in ten minutes and inspired all the rest.

They had never seen anything like it, United won away 5-1,
Another European Semi-Final made.
After playing such great football, to win it was surely on,
Only to lose semi final to Partisan Belgrade.
It seemed a cup that Matt Busby was destined never to win,
Came second in the league that year so had to wait again.

Won the league again in 67 so back in Europe once more,
For the only trophy to elude them so far.
They had twice won the league and the F.A. Cup for sure,
Now it was time to 'raise the bar.'
Especially as the final was in England in 1968,
To win it at Wembley would be an un-miss able date.

Sir Matt Busby C.B.E.

26-05-1909   9   20-01-1994

United beat teams from Malta, Sarajevo & Gornik of Poland,
To reach the semi final again.
Could they now go one further to strike up the band,
Drawn against Real from Spain.
Beat Real Madrid only 1-0 at home, but drew away three all,
At last they reach the Final, and a Wembley 'curtain call.'

A Wembley final against the Eagles of Lisbon again,
Eusebio the star of their bid.
Denis Law missing the match, in hospital, in pain.
Taking his place, the young Brian Kidd.
A goalless first half, neither side getting a grip,
Then Bobby Charlton scored with a rare headed flick.

One nil to United, but hands on the cup, not yet,
The United fans hold their breath.
But oh no, ten minutes to go and Benfica find the net
The Portuguese strong 'at the death.'
Then Eusebio through, alone on goal, only Stepney to beat,
Stepney makes a diving save and fans arise from their seat.

Extra time a few minutes old, a ball headed on to Best.
The winger started a dribbling run.
Rounded the keeper, scored, and was mobbed by the rest,
United now winning two one.
Two minutes later we had a goal from Brian Kidd,
Then a goal from Bobby Charlton that 'put on the lid.'

For Matt Busby its over, the dream is fulfilled,
The European Cup has been won.
Ten years from Munich, from the babes that were killed,
His work is almost done.
Over three decades he created three winning teams,
And Manchester United to be the club of dreams.

When he arrived at Old Trafford it was a bomb site mess,
Not even a pitch on which to play.
Now the club was not only the biggest, but the best,
And it was all his doing, you might say.
Man United are the best supported club in the land,
Playing great attacking football for the fans in the stand.

The first English club to win the European Cup,
Because he defied the English F.A.
United would never have played the teams from the top,
If he had accepted their wishes that day.
So Matt Busby we say thank you,............ you are the man,
You are Manchester United, you're how the beauty began

United Fever

I must go down to Old Trafford again,
To walk along Matt Busby Way,
To join the throng in red and white,
To watch United play.
Throbbing , heaving, bustling, weaving, getting carried along.
Listening to the fans chanting, and joining in the songs.

I must go down to Old Trafford again,
Hear the click of the old turnstyle.
Buy my programme just inside,
Then mill around for awhile.
Listening, talking, laughing, joining in with the football speak,
Then I climb a 'hundred' stairs, on the way to find my seat.

I must go down to Old Trafford again,
Gaze over the enlarging crowd,
Seats filling up so quickly,
Stretford End getting increasingly loud,
Roaring, clapping, supporting when the players do appear,
United kick off to start the match and, its one enormous cheer.

I must go down to Old Trafford again,
To see Man United score,
To rise in unison in our seats,
Add to the deafening roar.
Shouting, screaming, celebrating a beautiful headed goal,
Defensive play of opponents has finally taken its toll.

I must go down to Old Trafford again,
To celebrate a win,
To feel the glow you get inside,
When three points are counted in.
Climbing, rising, ascending the top of the premier league,
Reaching home after exciting day, yet feeling no fatigue.

Feb 6th 1958.

Munich as remembered by me as an eleven year old boy.

I remember it well, though just a boy,
Came out of school, so full of joy.
United were through, semi final made,
Battling draw at Red Star Belgrade.

We played football, without a care,
At the side of Liptons, on concrete square.
Against the wall I scored a goal,
What came next, scoured heart and soul.

Have you heard the news, some workers said,
United's plane has crashed, some players dead.
We all ran to the newsagents shop,
Is the news true, please say it's not.

We're not sure yet, the man replied
If the plane's crashed, or if anyone's died.
Could be a rumour, we're just not sure,
Switch on the tv. to find out more.

Ran down Rosebank Road as fast as I could,
To go straight home, would have been no good.
We didn't have a tele, but Aunty Florrie did.
These horrible rumours, I was desperate to rid.

She switched it on, flickering black and white,
The news came through and filled me with fright.
United's plane had crashed, it was all true.
Didn't know where to look, or what to do.

We heard the grim news, tears in my eyes.
These brilliant players, there were no goodbyes.
Going with my dad, I'd seen every home game.
Without United, it wouldn't be the same.

I walked to my home in Edenbridge Road,
My eyes welled up as my mum, I told.
Dad walked in, he'd heard the news too,
We turned on the Wireless, more news filtered through.

At Briscoe Lane next day, school was quiet,
Even at playtime, not the usual riot.
Can't really remember how we all got through,
Teachers and kids were all subdued

So quickly to go from joyful to sad,
It was hard to remember the joy that we'd had.
Seven great Reds lost their lives in that snow,
Then fifteen days later, big Duncan to go.

Two other Reds never played again,
What a lot to lose, a team of great men.
Ten football players, coach and trainer too
Would never again, lace a football shoe

Jimmy Murphy took over, time didn't stand still.
He took Bobby and Dennis, Harry and Bill.
Added a few kids to those that were left
And started again, from the worlds biggest theft.

Signed Quixall and Setters, reached Cup Final that year.
Once more the fans had something to cheer.
But it was all done on an emotional tide.
And a Cup Final defeat ended the glorious ride.

One thing though that Murphy showed,
The end of United hadn't been told.
Eventually Busby came back to the helm,
To rebuild a team that would overwhelm.
Manchester United would reach the heights again.
More great teams build with great football men.
But now as we join in, with the fans raves,
We still say, Thank you…. for the Busby Babes.

Bobby Charlton

If Manchester United are wearing the 'glamour gown,'
Then Bobby Charlton must be the 'jewel in the crown.'
Arguably the most loved footballer ever to play the game,
No man more humble, yet no man with more fame.

A survivor of the Munich Air Crash on that fateful day,
And overcoming the trauma, he continued to play.
An attacking player who loved to run with the ball,
Able to beat a man with ,seemingly, no effort at all.

He played football with a smile on his face,
He made it look easy, always played with such grace.
He'd run at opponents, could shoot with either foot,
And score a great goal, more often than not.

If he was fouled, he shrugged and just carried on,
When Bobby was playing, all malice was gone.
Played over 700 games, only once was he booked,
Even then the ref rescinded it, and it was, overlooked.

Got 106 caps for England, scored forty nine goals,
Playing mostly on the wing, or from the midfield hole.
A mainstay of the team, played in three World Cups,
And when we won it at Wembley, with tears held it up.

That was Bobby, emotive, the smiles and the tears,
He won English and European Player of the Year.
But ready to give credit to the rest of his side,
Had great humility, but wore his shirt with pride.

United won the European Cup in Nineteen Sixty Eight,
Exactly ten years from Munich, it had been a long wait.
Matt was delighted and again Bobby cried,
They won it for the manager, the tears they couldn't hide.

He played United's first team football from 1956 to 73,
Plus 106 games for England, some talent there you see.
Whenever he got the ball, a buzz went round the crowd,
They sensed something special, he made them feel proud.

He won every honour that the modern game could give,
Extolled the virtues of the game, made his football live.
Never once was disciplined, never once stepped out of line,
Never once suspended, or even get a fine.

So thank you Sir Bobby, for enriching our great game,
Playing beautiful football, without a hint of shame.
He is still there at United, which just says it all,
The Clubs greatest ambassador for our game of football.

Georgie Best

Bob Bishop the United Scout, phoned Matt Busby one day,
Said "I think I've got you a genius, you need to see him play."
"He's from Belfast, Northern Ireland, and his name is George Best,"
Well he was only fifteen years of age, but what a 'treasure chest.'

Made his debut at seventeen in September Sixty Three.
Made the most of his dribbling skills and fans said "he'll do for me."
Scored his first, two games later, and the lad was on his way,
The Burnley fullback marking him was turned 'inside out' that day.

He played seventeen times that season, and he scored six goals,
Not bad for a teenager, who dragged fullbacks over't coals.
The fans already loved him, knew he would be a big star,
The ball seemed to stay at his feet, as though it was stuck with tar.

A 'regular' the next season, and increased goal tally as well,
Bestie improving all the time and the 'time was beginning to tell.'
United won the league again, and George had 'come of age,'
In the European Cup once more, and for Best a bigger Stage.

In Europe, United played Benfica in quarter final stage,
Won only 3-2 at home, then Bestie 'opened another page.'
In Lisbon they named him El Beatle because of his long hair,
In fact he had a blinder, scored two and the Reds won 5-1 there.

El Beatle was a good name, because of his pop-star looks,
His fame increasing all the time, they couldn't fill enough books.
Scored more goals again this year, already made his name,
In fact, the once shy, homesick Irishman is the biggest in the game.

Busby dropped him for a match, the press said "won't be the same,"
"Too cocky," He said, "beats him, then comes & beats him again."
United won the league again, this time by four points clear,
Into Europe once again, could this be the telling year?

Its 1968 and United are in the European Cup Final at last,
At Wembley against Benfica, old enemies of the past.
Score one all and extra time, Bestie gets the ball,
A mazy run around the keeper, scores, and Benfica 'hit the wall.'

Then Kidd with a header, and a Bobby Charlton special,
The score is now 4-1, and Benfica have lost their mettle.
We've done it, the first English team to win the European Cup,
After many years of trying,............ they finally get to lift it up.

Uniteds finest hour had come, with Best an all important part,
Scored 32 goals that season, and that's just for a start.
Won both European and English, 'Footballer of the year,'
Is Best, United's finest ever player? If not, he must be near.

Best is now a celebrity, the first football 'superstar,'
With mega bucks and pop star looks, 'how I wonder what you are.'
Opens a Fashion Boutique, and Nightclub, is his eye still on the ball?
Football player or a celebrity? Its now 'too close to call.'

He's still filling the newspapers, banner headlines are unfurled,
Less to do with football, more George Best and Miss World.
Still playing good football though, still got precocious skill,
Still getting kicked a lot, as defenders move in for't kill.

Late sixties, early seventies still playing forty games a season,
The games that he doesn't play, suspension being the reason.
Though he came back from suspension once, and added to his fame,
Played a cup tie at Northampton , and scored 6 goals in one game.

In season seventy two - seventy three Best only played four games,
Started going 'missing,'......... he just did not want to train.
Alcohol was, by now, beginning to have an influence on his mind,
He wanted a sort of release from life, football had become a 'bind.'

Bestie played his last game for United on 'New Years Day' 1974
He was only twenty seven, could have given so much more.
But its certain that United had the best years of his life,
Some beautiful football moments, before the 'booze put in the knife.'

So a big Thank You Georgie, for the ten seasons that we had,
A pure football genius, who drove opposing fullbacks mad.
I'm just glad that I saw you, as you so graced the game,
And now that your not with us, football is not the same.

The King of the Stretford End

"Denis Law King" the Stretford End used to shout,
When he'd scored a goal, or given opponent a clout.
Quicksilver, Blond Bomber, The Lawman, a few of his names,
But one thing was certain, he excelled at the game.

The son of a trawlerman from the city of Aberdeen,
One of the greatest footballers Scotland has seen.
If you'd seen him as a boy, it didn't always look that way,
Had a squint in his eye, and a little frail you might say.

But he didn't let his shortcomings bring him down,
He practised his football, to be the best in town.
Played first team at Huddersfield at the age of 16,
He started getting noticed by First Division teams.

Man City signed him for Fifty Five Thousand Pounds,
He played against Luton, in an F.A. Cup Third Round.
He scored six, then the ref abandoned the game,
Which after scoring six goals, you'd call it a shame.

To make matters worse, they lost the replay 3-1,
Law scored that goal, but the Cup was gone.
So Denis Law scored 7, he was a good catch,
And they still ended up losing the match.

He then signed for Torino in the Italian League,
Scored goals but defensive play, made him leave.
Matt Busby had wanted him and admired from afar,
He paid a record £115,000 and it got him a star.

Denis signed for United in Nineteen Sixty Two,
Scored 29 goals in his first season, it's true.
Helped get to Cup Final and Leicester they beat,
The club was at last getting back on it's feet.

The rest of the Sixties became the clubs glory years,
Won the league twice, and European Cup to cheer.
He won European Player of the year in Nineteen Sixty Four,
The only Scottish player to 'walk through that door.

He scored 237 goals for United and played over 400 games,
A fantastic player and fans always chanted his name.
A fiery Scot who often got into trouble with the referee,
He'd get suspended at Christmas, so home for Hogmanay.

Played over fifty times for his beloved national team,
But a consequence was an injury that spoiled his future dreams.
Knee operations and explorations consistently gave him pain,
Missed the European cup Final, ...in hospital again.

But Denis Law will always be, in United's Hall of Fame,
A part of the glory, often feisty, never tame.
'Denis Law King' will always be remembered with pride,
A big part of 'Best, Law and Charlton,' the great trio of the side.

As a fan in the sixties, what a great team to recant,
And Denis Law King was the United fans chant.
The King of the Stretford end, the man from Aberdeen,
One of the best players, Man United fans have seen.

Brian Robson

Tough as granite but shone like marble,
That's Brian Robson our Captain Marvel.
Possibly even too brave, was the lad,
Probably the greatest captain that we ever had.

Born and raised in Chester le Street,
Grew up always with a ball at his feet.
Trialled with Newcastle but not taken on,
Moved from home and signed for West Brom.

Made his debut in Nineteen Seventy Five season,
Progress halted for a very good reason.
Broke his leg three times in a year,
Battled back strongly, showing little fear.

When Ron Atkinson came to manage United,
One West Brom player really made him excited.
He knew he was good, cause he'd seen him grow,
And he knew at United that his class would show.

So age twenty four, Robson came to the Reds,
Soon became captain, he had an 'old head.'
The red fans loved him, love a man with fight,
Bossed the midfield, and made defence tight.

For United he played over four hundred times,
Scored one hundred goals, a record sublime.
For England he's received ninety caps,
Would have been more but for injury mishaps.

Robson had stamina, aggression, fearless in tackle,
A goal-scorers intuition and loved a battle.
A great captain, a man born to lead.
That beautiful player that every team needs.

Captain Marvel became England's 'Lionheart,'
A football British Bulldog always ready to 'bark.'
When we look at Brian Robson, we look on with pride,
Because this man would always 'grace any side.'

Mickey Thomas

When I was twelve we moved to Colwyn Bay,
I was only twelve, so I didn't have any say.
Grew up there, went to Pendorlan School,
Still loved United and the whole school knew.
Used to 'bunk' last lesson to watch midweek game,
Last train home, then more to tell, of United fame.

I tell you this because of a player we signed,
A tricky little winger, United's favourite kind.
Signed him from Wrexham 'when they were good,'
United fans loved him, as they always would.
They love a player who beats opponents and excites the fan,
And Mickey Thomas from Mochdre, was this kind of man.

United signed him in Nineteen Seventy Eight,
And to see him for United I just couldn't wait.
You see he grew up in the Colwyn Bay scene,
He even played for my old school team.
So Mickey Thomas was my favourite player for a time,
When the fans chanted his name, for me it was sublime.

Mickey only played for us for three short years,
A fast tricky winger who played without fear.
But in that time, he played in 110 games,
And scored fifteen goals and so added to his fame.
He was capped for his country over fifty times as well,
Scored in a win against England, of which he loves to tell.

He won an F.A. Cup Runner Up medal in 1979,
United cruelly robbed in the last minute of time.
So thank you Mickey for the breath of fresh air,
In a defensive period under Dave Sexton's 'care.'
He motored up and down that wing like 'Ayrton Senna,'
But if you meet him, don't ever borrow a 'tenner.'
Seriously though, he was a player of United's kind,
From Colwyn Bay a great football find.
A busy little player who played with such zest,
And a real crowd favourite with the United crest.

The Best of all Time

Sir Alex Ferguson, the fiery Scot,
As a manager, best of the lot.
Won ten trophies with Aberdeen
Then came to England, to re-ignite a team
From Man. United, the invite came,
Since that day, it's not been the same.

Though slow at first, it soon picked up.
His first United trophy, the F.A. Cup
Then the trickle turned into a flow,
And 20 years later, 33 trophies on show.
Great football, great players, they've passed the test,
And as for the manager, he's out won the rest.

We don't care about the 'Beckham Boot'
And facing the 'Hairdryer' we don't give a hoot.
He's the man with the consoling arm,
And when it warrants, he lays on the charm.
Eric? Van Nystleroy? players arrive, players leave,
He just wins more trophies, more 'stripes' on his sleeve.

Won more Premier Leagues than any other man,
And while he's been manager, five F.A. Cups in the can.
Not to mention two Champions Leagues,
His teams win trophies with relative ease.
The most successful manager our team's ever had
When he retires other teams won't be sad.

So carry on Fergy, may you never alter.
Because you are our own 'Rock of Gibraltar'
And with the Rock in place, we know we've a chance,
Of seeing this great club, all the more enhanced.
All other managers, stand in line,
Salute Sir Alex, the best of all time.

My Football Team

Why is it that Poets are mean
When it comes to writing about the football scene,
I would like to tell you of my team.

I've been going to watch them since 10 years old,
With my Dad at first, it must be told,
And there's always been more highs than lows.

Weaned on Byrne, Colman, Edwards and Pegg,
These Busby babes put teams to bed,
Plus pioneers in Europe it has to be said.

After Munich, there was Charlton, Law and Best,
How could I ever support the rest,
My team could ever ,only, be the Reds.

They've always had the most flair ever,
And so my ties I couldn't sever,
United always, Man City never.

Then Giggsy, Beckham and Paul Scholes,
Always ready to score great goals,
With players like these, there's no 'black holes.'

And now we see Fletcher, Rooney, Valencia too,
 If one doesn't score, another will do,
And Van Der Sar keeps clean sheet for you.

They play the game just to excite,
Their quick passing style fills teams with fright,
Overwhelm with attacking might.

Man United set out to score,
Leave the fans just wanting more,
Other teams are a defensive bore.

So this is why I love my team,
The greatest team you've ever seen,
Because they fulfil my every dream.

Ryan Giggs

This is the story of Ryan Giggs,
Moved from Cardiff to Swinton when he was six.
Captained English Schools as a boy,
But he knew that to play for Wales, would be his real joy.
Trained with Man City when just fourteen,
But to get his signature, Fergie was keen.
Went round to his house and the deal was done,
And City's boy became United's son.
Good job Fergie was on his toes,
Pinched from under Man City's nose.

Won the Youth Cup with the Nevilles, Beckham, Scholes,
In his full first team debut he scored a goal.
He had such pace with his frame so lean,
Up and down the wing like a well oiled machine
He twisted and turned like a fairground ride,
Till fullbacks thought, they were twisted inside.
Became a favourite at just seventeen,
The fans loved him and the girls 'mad keen.'
The new 'George Best' was his fan given name,
And 20 years later still gracing the game.

He's won more trophies than any other player,
Played all over Europe, from Moscow to Marbella.
Scored goals in every single Premiership season
A record that can never, ever be beaten.
Against Arsenal scored the best ever F.A. cup goal,
The gunners demolished in heart and soul.
Remember that goal, as he turned away from the rest,
Shirt twirling around, above hairy chest.
That goal celebration, fans will never forget,
But its good to know, he's not finished yet.

In Premier League icons, Ryan Giggs is top of them all,
He has everything a player needs, his c.v. stands tall.
Speed, skill, flair, application, and a real desire,
Loyalty, a love for his club, not the biggest buyer.
He has got Manchester United in his heart,
With nigh on 800 appearances just for a start.
He has won every trophy that the game can offer,
But with his dedication, always looking for another.
And so Giggsy we salute your winning ways,
A Man United legend through all of your days.

He's won the Premier League ten times in all,
With four F.A. cup final wins, he's well on the ball.
And two League cup final wins in addition to these,
To win Champions League final, twice, is not to be sneezed.
Not to mention twice P.F.A. young player of the year,
And an O.B.E. for services to football, its clear.
That this young man has won more than all before,
Even than footballing legends from days of yore.
Probably more to come, he's still playing the game,
I think its fair to say, Ryan Giggs has made his own name.

David Beckham

This is the story of a London boy,
Playing football was his only ploy.
Teachers asked him, "what do you want to be? "
A professional footballer, answered he.
They smiled and said, "he'll live and learn,"
But he was determined to be a star turn.
Tottenham Hotspur noticed his skills,
But it was Man United who gave him his thrills.
He went to a Bobby Charlton Soccer School week,
Bobby said to Fergie, "come and take a peek."
So he signed on for his favourite team,
That's how it happened, the start of his dream.

His first success, the F.A. Youth Cup scene,
Scored in the final, against a 'London' team.
Then a league title for United Reserves,
This team of young stars only got their deserves.
Then he went on loan to Preston North End,
Scored direct from a corner, to set a trend.
They loved him there, recognised his potential,
But young Becks, only saw United, essential.
Came back to Old Trafford, played against Port Vale,
His first League Cup debut, to start the tale.
He was on his way, to prove those teachers wrong,
Going to be a star, and it would not be long.

Made his Premier League Debut in April 95,
A nil-nil draw that didn't come alive.
But the story really starts in the new season,
No new signings, for some strange reason.
Big names had left that Fergie didn't replace,
Cos he had good youngsters in whom he had faith,
But they lost the first game at the 'Villa', 3-1,
Critics and fans thought Fergie had 'gone.'
"You'll never win anything with kids in the side,"
Said Alan Hansen with his usual pride.
But Beckham and co. made him 'eat his words.'
Won the League and Cup Double, just for a first.

On the very first day of the following season,
Beckham received instant fame, for this reason.
He spotted Neil Sullivan way off his line,
And thought he'll never, ever, get back in time.
So from inside his own half, he fired in a shot,
The keeper, left stranded and stumbling a lot,
Could only watch as, in the net the ball whizzed,
Like Pele's world cup shot, 'except Pele missed.'
It was voted by some as the best goal ever.
But Beckham wasn't afraid to try something clever.
United won the Premier League twice in two years,
And Becks voted Young Player of the Year, by his peers.

In the 98-99 season David Beckham won the treble,
With his mates, Giggsy, Scholsey and Gary Neville.
Premier League, Champions League, F.A. Cup too,
Wonder if those teachers now accept it as true.
He really has become that star turn,
With a pop-star wife and 'money to burn.'
A celebrity lifestyle that's all very nice,
Lives in a mansion after marrying Posh Spice.
T.V commitments, adverts and interviews too,
Each year that passes, more 'celeb' stuff to do.
On these other commitments, Fergie's not keen,
Should be football foremost, not the glamour scene.

United won the Premier League three years on the trot,
They were successful, the team was so hot.
Now United fans adored David Becks.
And its true that Beckham loved the Reds.
But 'Team Beckham' had become bigger than the club,
That's why Fergie had to sell him, that was the rub.
So reluctantly Becks signed for Real Madrid,
Never wanted to leave, he was a United kid.
Thought he'd be at United for his football life,
Probably would have been except for his 'trouble & strife'.
But United fans put all the 'celeb' stuff to bed,
To them David Beckham will always be a Red.

King Eric the Red

Ooh aah Cantona, the Man United football star,
That arrogant stance,
That surly glance,
That Kung Fu dance,
Oh how we love the man from France.

Ooh aah Cantona, the Man United football star,
That touch on the ball,
That collar stood tall,
That guttural call,
Oh how we love the man from Gaul.

Ooh aah Cantona, the Man. United football star,
That player of the year with the P.F.A
Those solitary strikes in the games away,
That he's the catalyst of this teams great play,
Oh how we love the man from Marsaille.

Ooh aah Cantona, the Man United football Star,
To other players, the balls he feeds,
For the Reds, this man bleeds,
He has met, all this teams needs,
Oh how we're glad we 'stole' him from Leeds.

Ooh aah Cantona, the Man. United football star,
That complete lack of bling,
That seagull-trawler poetic thing,
That the fans still love to sing,
Ooh aah Cantona, to our Football King.

The Worlds Best Goalkeeper

I wonder if Fergie really knew what he had found,
When he signed a keeper for half a million pounds.
Peter Boleslaw Schmeichel was the keepers name,
And United's defence would never again be the same.
At Six feet Four inches an absolute giant of a man,
Would 'bawl' at his defenders to keep them on plan.

Played for Brondby, a Danish first division side,
Had won the Danish League, four seasons out of five.
Had already played for the Danish National team,
And a U.E.F.A Cup semi final with Brondby, it seems.
But no fan had heard of him when he signed for the Reds,
Well Fergie had, but would he stand the test?

In Schmeichel's first season United finished runners up,
But for the first time ever, won the Football League Cup.
The fans all loved him, right from the start,
They knew in the teams success, he'd play a big part.
With Denmark he won the Euro tournament that year,
And was voted the World's Best Goalkeeper, he had no peer.

And so The Great Dane became United's number one,
He stood the test all right, all doubting was gone.
Won Premier League, with Schmeichel's 22 clean sheets,
First league title for 26 years, so no mean feat.
Once again named World's Best Keeper in 1993,
Fergie knew what he'd done when he signed him you see.

Schmeichel started attacks with his famous long throw,
He'd kick the ball into opponents penalty area you know.
Even scored a goal against Rotor Volgograd,
Went up for a corner, ………they say goalkeepers are mad!
Saved a Bergkamp penalty in the last minute of time,
Won the Cup and League with European still on line.

So United won the Treble in Nineteen Ninety Nine,
With a Peter Schmeichel cartwheel in celebration time.
The "Bargain of the Century," said Fergie that year,
And after eight years at the top, Schmeichel said "cheers."
At age of thirty five, the Great Dane moved on with a tear,
But Red fans know, the Best Keeper in the World, was here!

Judgement Day

Sunday 12th May 2008-Wigan v Man Utd /Chelsea v Bolton
Level on points, last game of season.

We've gone all season, now it's judgement day,
It's the final curtain, the final say.
The colours on the Trophy, what will they be,
The red of Manchester or the blue of Chelsea?
Its kick-off time, let the battle begin,
Who'll be the Champions, the trophy to win?

United kick off, Chelsea are late.
Perhaps they're afraid of their impending fate.
Or perhaps its another Avram mind game,
He's got to have something on which to put blame.
They get an early chance, Drogba's on side!
But oh dear me, he's put it wide.

It's quarter past three, John Terry's in pain,
Dislocated elbow - miss the rest of the game.
What will they do without central defender?
On comes Alex - the Great Pretender.
Over at Wigan, United fans rejoice,
Rooney fouled in the box by Emmerson Boyce.

Up steps Ronaldo - pressure's on to score,
Cool as ever in the heat of the war,
Its Wigan nil, United one,
Surely without Terry, Chelsea's gone.
If it stays like this, the Premiership is Red,
And poor old Chelsea are good as dead.

But it's only half-time and the battle's still on,
Its still very tense, cos nothing's yet won.
Chelsea make changes. Shevchenko's on't pitch,
But he's hardly scored. So that's a bit rich.
The games carry on with nerves a bit raw,
There's nothing friendly, its all out war.

All of a sudden, there's a big change,
Can you believe it, Shevchenko's found range?
Players rejoice, the Chelsea fans roar,
Shevchenko has actually managed to score.
Now its different, what will the Reds do?
If Wigan score, the Premierships Blue.

Over at Wigan, the mobiles carry the tale,
And United fans start to bite fingernail.
Then Rooney gets the ball and sees Giggs in space,
And passes the ball at just the right pace,
Its such a good pass, Giggs got time in hand,
He strokes it perfect, past the beaten Kirkland.

Let celebrations begin, it must now be won,
Only ten minutes to go, the work is done.
And at Stamford Bridge, Chelsea really are gone,
Bolton have equalised, they've gone and got one!
The Bridge is silent - Chelsea fans groan,
United have finally hammered it home!

The Champions League Final May 21 2008

It's the Champions League Final Two Thousand and Eight,
The easternmost venue so far to date.
Held over in Moscow, Stadium Luzhniki,
Some fans think, they're taking the 'mickey'.

The rest of us say, we really don't care,
As long as we're in it, as long as we're there.
An all English final, the first time ever,
A Man Utd double? Never say never.

So its Utd verses Chelsea, top two in the Prem,
Both massive football clubs, locking horns again.
Utd won the premiership, so Fergie up for't double,
If Chelsea lose this one, Avram's up for trouble.

The match kicks off at Ten Forty Five,
Twenty one minutes before game comes alive.
Scholesy and Makelele with clash of heads,
Both get booked, Scholesy's face bloody red.

A few minutes later, with cotton wool up his nose,
A quick one-two with Wes, and away the back goes.
Wes Brown delivers a delightful left foot ball,
Ronaldo rises high in the box, is he nine foot tall?

It's a beautiful header and it's one nil to us,
Both Essien and Cech are on the wrong bus.
Then Ballack gets a chance, when Rio's pushed in't back
It's nearly an own goal but Edwin's on't right track.

It's straight back down t'other end with a 70yd Rooney pass,
Ronaldo controls the ball and skips along the grass.
His perfect cross is goal bound, from Tevez diving head,
Cech makes amends this time and pushes it out instead.

The move isn't over yet as Carrick follows in,
Its got to be another goal, in this game we want to win.
Either side of keeper, and United fans will rave,
But its straight down the middle,and Cech makes the save.

Rooney sends in a perfect cross, a few minutes later on,
Makelele just cannot reach, but surely Tevez can,
Carlos slides along the ground, just to touch it in,
Misses it completely and a chance begs again.

Three nil up at half time is what the score should be,
For how we've played and chances made, it wouldn't be flattery.
At least make it to the break with a clean sheet for sure,
But a twice deflected, miss hit shot and Lampard free to score.

So instead of victory by half-time, we now go in one all.
Its not what we envisaged as we played such great football.
We really hammered Chelsea, yet still anybodies game,
Will the tide turn in second half and Chelsea reach for fame.

Chelsea come out second half, inspired by the score,
They start to play good football, and now the blue fans roar.
We can win this now you blues, and it's not an empty boast,
For Drogba shoots from 20yds, but it rebounds off the post.

Its now United to defend, with Chelsea on the rise.
Good attacking football, reaching for the skies.
Blue waves surge across the field, time and time again.
It's nearly end of time, we must hold out till then.

Fergie makes a substitution, with just three minutes left,
Giggs on for Scholesy, can he make a difference yet?
It's a great significance, cos its Giggsy,s record game,
One appearance more than 'Bobby' of old United fame.

So now we go to extra time, this tie's not over yet,
Who's going to be the winner, I wouldn't like to bet.
The first chance goes to Chelsea, they find the door ajar,
Good interplay inside the box and Lampard hits the bar.

Then United get opportunity, as this tie seesaws,
Giggsy has a glorious chance to make the red fans roar.
He hits his shot towards the goal, but Terry twists mid-air,
And somehow gets his head to ball, and puts red fans in despair.

Tevez and Ballack both get booked 4 minutes from the whistle,
Players run from everywhere, hone in like guided missile.
Drogba is a silly boy, he gives us all a laugh,
He slaps Vidic across the face, and gets an early bath.

The ref. blows to end the match, but its not over yet,
Its now penalty shootout time, and red and blue get set.
The referee is ready, goalkeepers both shake hands,
How many shots will hit the net, how many hit the stand.

Tevez, Ballack, Carrick, Bellitti all make the score two all.
Ronaldo steps up to the spot, then weakly hits the ball.
Cech diving to his right saves the ball with ease,
Ronaldo holds his head in hands and falls down to his knees.

Lampard takes the next and scores, that puts them in the lead,
Hargreaves keeps his nerve to get the leveller they need.
Ashley Cole makes a weak shot, but somehow in it goes,
Nani makes the score four all to keep Chelsea on their toes.

Just one more pen to take and its Terry for the blues,
If the Chelsea captain scores this one, then United lose.
We will win the Champions League was Avrams proudest boast,
But Terry slips as he hits the ball, and it cannons off the post.

United fans roar, "we're still in the game,"
Terry's tears flow as he holds head in shame.
Its five pens each, and the score is four all,
And now its sudden death, winner taking all.

Excitement now at fever pitch, who will get this cup?
Another five pens each, before this game is up.
Some fans just cannot look, others hold their breath,
Who ever misses now, for them it's sudden death.

Anderson takes the first, and it's now five four,
Kalou for the blues and Chelsea, level once more.
It's now record maker Giggs and he tucks his pen away,
Up steps 'Le Sulk' and Van der Sar wins the day.

It's all over, we've won it, the cup with the big ears,
John Terry can't believe it, his face awash with tears.
Red fans jumping up and down, players and staff go wild,
Fergies only done it again, another Double winning side.

Scholesy

Paul Aaron Scholes as a football star, an enigma unique,
Doesn't seek the limelight or the praise of his physique.
Not for him the interviews, the glamour of T.V,
A very quiet person who shuns publicity.

But Scholesy plays for United, the biggest and the best,
Over six hundred appearances, so surely stood the test.
Scored nigh on one hundred and fifty goals,
From playing mostly in a supporting midfield role.

A local boy from Middleton, at United since fourteen,
A member of United's successful youth team scene.
Scored both goals on his first team debut match,
A 2-1 win against Port Vale, 'the door was now unlatched.'

In 95-96 United won the double and Paul played in 36,
He scored fourteen goals, and a first team place is fixed.
Now firmly a fan's favourite, but still the quiet type.
He's now worshipped by thousands, but doesn't like the hype.

One of his attributes is that he hardly ever 'gifts the ball,'
Always 'shows' in midfield, ready to heed the call.
Not the best 'tackler,' of that you can be sure,
Except for miss-timed tackles, he'd have played many more.

He is an amazing footballer, at top level for fourteen years,
A shy reserved family man, but acknowledges fans cheers.
A sufferer of asthma, but doesn't let it show,
The way he bosses the midfield, no one would ever know.

Paul Scholes has won Nine Premierships and Three F.A. Cups,
Two Champions Leagues and the list goes up and up.
Twenty Three in all, not bad for one so unassuming,
A one club man who's love for the Reds is really all consuming.

Already retired from England, his career is coming to its close,
But he'll boss a few more midfields yet, before he finally goes.
A Man United Legend, midfield redhead who is Paul Scholes,
Sprayed forty five yard passes and scored wonder goals.

FIFA Club World Cup Japan 2008

When America was adjusting to Barak Obama
United was adjusting to Japan.
Nine hours difference in Yokohama,
Will the proverbial hit the fan?

Surely it's too tiring, everybody said,
Coping with different time zones,
This will put your premiership to bed,
You'll be down to 'Harry's bare bones'.

But Fergie wasn't listening to this negative talk,
He said "we'll win it if we can",
Players said "we're 'United', lets, 'walk the walk',"
The team determined to a man.

With all the winners of FIFA's confederations.
The tournament had all it's best teams,
But who would finalise the celebrations,
Without coming apart at the seams?

As champions of Europe United received,
Free passage to the semi final round.
Only two possible games, so Fergie relieved,
And believed the cup was Manchester bound.

Gamba Osaka was the first team they met,
The Oceania Champions League winners,
Five times United hit the back of the net,
Making them look like beginners.

In the last five minutes, Osaka scored twice,
Making 5-3 look a respectable score.
For United it was all rather nice,
Because a final was made once more.

And so now into the Cup Final game,
Against a team from South America.
Opponents 'Liga de Quito' is the name,
The best team we've played by far.

The game is tight and we know it's hard,
And at half time the score is nil-nil .
But in the 49th minute Vidic gets a red card,
And it can only get harder still.

The team digs in and the ten men attack,
And into the net the ball is curled.
Wayne Rooney the master, to his best is back,
Now United sit 'on top of the world'

It's over, we've done it, it's time to celebrate,
The players get the cup in their hands.
The FIFA world club cup 2008,
Is on it's way to England.

The Race for the Premiership. 2009
Ten games to go.

Man United 1, Liverpool 4
The premiership gone? Have they shown us the door?
Is this the start? Have United cracked?
Or just a blip, will they be back?

Ten games to go, only four points in it,
Can Chelsea or Liverpool go on and win it?
We'll all just have to wait and see,
As to who will finish on the top of the tree.

Nine games to go, United lose again,
2-0 away to Fulham, and finish with 9 men
Liverpool win again, so lead is cut to one,
But Chelsea lose to Spurs, perhaps they too have gone.

Scousers play on Saturday, win with last minute strike,
Puts them two points in front, United now must fight.
Chelsea win as well so the pressures really on,
United play Aston Villa, nearly lose the game 2-1.

I think it's now all over, but then Ronaldo scores,
A great equaliser, but we need a winning goal of course,
Still win the Premiership? Now I'm a believer,
Because of a 17 year old Italian called Kiko Macheda.

Eight games to go and all three teams win their game,
United still one point in front, position just the same.
Liverpool are playing well, they think Utd's built on sand,
But don't forget United's still got a game in hand.

Seven games to go, and Liverpool only draw,
A home game 'gainst Arsenal that finishes 4 all.
United beat the Portsmouth with the score 2 nil,
Chelsea draw at home as well, so United leaders still.

Three points clear United now and still got game in hand,
But with 6 games still to play, don't yet strike up the band.
Tough games ahead, perhaps still changes at the top,
Liverpool not yet given up, no tears yet on the kop.

Liverpool and Chelsea both win early on,
United with late kick off so the pressures really on.
Half time arrives with United 0-2 down,
The reds are under water, is this the day they drown.

The second half gets started, on comes Tevez & Scholes,
Now some stunning football, and United get 5 goals.
So from 2nil down at half time, the reds kill fatted calf,
Three points clear and game in hand, what a second half.

United win at Middlesboro, Chelsea win as well,
Liverpool win on Sunday, so not a lot to tell.
United still got 4 games left, the other two only 3,
Still 3 points up, with game in hand, one hand on trophy.

Liverpool win on Saturday, 3-0 at West Ham,
They go back to the top, piling on the jam.
United beat Man City 2-0 without a fight,
Three points clear again, and, regain bragging rights.

United just got 3 games left, four points is all they need,
If they win midweek, will be only 1 point for the league.
They play at Wigan on Wednesday, United's game in hand,
One nil down at half time, loud cheers in scouser land.

A good thing about United, never know when they're beat,
A back heel flick from Tevez and Fergies off his seat.
Ten minutes to go, and the score is still one all.
Edge of the box shot from Carrick, now hear United roar.

United need one point if Liverpool win both games,
A draw will do gainst Arsenal for more premiership fame.
We've done it, its ours , we've gone and got the draw,
Who cares what Liverpool do, Premiership's ours for sure.

And we've won it at Old Trafford, celebrate at home,
Now we can concentrate, on our little trip to Rome.
We've won it with a game in hand, infuriate scousers so,
And to add insult to injury, its three times in a row.
We've won the league title now 18 times in all,
Equalled Liverpool's record, no wonder they are sore.

Cristiano Ronaldo dos Santos Aveiras

Born on a Portuguese island in the Atlantic Ocean,
A young boy grew up with one main notion.
To be a great footballer was the outstanding thing,
And Cristiano Ronaldo became the 'step-over king.'
He was called Ronaldo for no football reason,
But because dad's favourite actor was Ronald Reagan.

Sporting Lisbon was his first professional team,
And dribbling trickery was his football theme.
He worked hard to be a master of the ball,
And at age sixteen he got the first team call.
Scored two goals against Moreirense in his debut game,
And it didn't take long to make famous his name.

They opened a new stadium and he was delighted,
Because the inaugural game was against Man United.
He had a chance to show just what he could do,
To show them his tricks and maybe beat one or two.
United defenders said, "Fergie please sign this guy,"
We can't get the ball off him, that's the reason why.

That friendly was in August Two thousand and three,
And Fergie listens to his players you see.
He got his signature for Twelve million pounds,
And at age 18 he'd got best young player around.
Came on as a sub. in the seasons very first game,
And his Bolton opponent had never known such pain.

The red fans took to him like a 'duck to water,'
Opposing fullbacks were like 'lambs to slaughter.'
Hadn't seen anything like it since the great George Best,
Only young, but stood the greatest test.
Scored his first goal for United from a free kick,
Developed a free kick technique that just seemed to 'click.'

In 2005 he was voted ' Young player of the Year,'
He could head, dribble, and he would shoot without fear.
Won two consecutive Barclay Player of the Month awards
Was now scoring regularly for the Man United cause
His fiftieth Red goal is a nice story to tell you,
Because he scored his fiftieth against the boys in 'sky blue'.

United won the Premier League after a four year wait,
With Ronaldo scoring 23 goals, his best season to date.
Rumours abound that Real Madrid want him to sign,
But Fergie gives him new contract to keep him in line.
Made him the highest paid player in the teams history,
But as for the future, …………he is the 'man of mystery.'

He increased his goal tally again in the very next year,
Great goal scoring for a winger, it's clear.
Won the Champions League and Premier League Double,
He scored 42 goals to put the rest in trouble.
In scoring so many, he won another accolade, its true,
First winger to win the European Golden Shoe.

Real Madrid again increased Fergie's fury,
Enticing Ronaldo to join the Real Madrid story.
They knew that he would like to join them one day,
But again Fergie managed to persuade him to stay.
One more season and maybe with a little luck,
We can be the first to retain the Champions League Cup.

He missed the first two months of the next season,
Ankle surgery in Amsterdam being the reason.
Scored his first league goal at the end of September,
And the best Champions League goal that I can remember.
A forty yard 'special' against Porto, the Portuguese team.
Got us through to the Semi Final to continue the dream.

He upset Fergie by showing dissent when 'subbed,'
Is his egomania getting too big for the club?
Some fans are saying "his heart is not in it,"
But he's still scoring goals, still trying to win it.
Fergie has seen it all before, and he won't bend,
But is this for Ronaldo, 'the beginning of the end.'

The Champions League Final was disappointing for all,
United looked like they needed 'a wake up call.'
Against Barcelona, we lost it by two goals to nil,
As for retaining the cup, it seems we didn't have the will.
In June 2009, United accepted Real's 80 million pound fee,
And United fans realise that this has to be.
We can thank Ronaldo for six wonderful seasons,
But we can only accept the eighty million reasons.

Ole Gunnar Solskjaer

When United couldn't score but doing all the attacking,
Fergie always had another ploy.
He'd send on Solksjaer, the 'Baby faced Assassin,'
And he'd score a goal, that Norwegian Boy.

Ole did his National Service, Norwegian Army way'
Though he didn't look old enough.
Whilst there he played part-time for Clausenengen F.K.
Norwegian Third Division was rough.

But it wasn't too tough for our Ole Gunnar,
He still managed to score lots of goals.
Scoring 17 goals in six Cup games, was a stunner,
He dragged defences over the coals.

The Norwegian Premier League then took note,
Ole signed for a team called Molde.
In his first season he 'sailed out in the boat,'
And 'sailed in with twenty goals.'

After scoring thirty one goals for Molde F.K.
Ole signed on for United.
Fergies One and a Half Million Pounds held sway,
And Sir Alex was delighted.

In his debut game against Blackburn Rovers,
Fergie sent him on as a sub.
After six minutes all the waiting was over
Ole scored with his very first touch.

He scored nineteen goals in his very first season,
And United won the league again.
His shooting was so accurate, that was the reason,
On target with nine out of ten.

He was a master at sitting on the bench,
And studying the style of play.
Then Fergie would call, and say 'no offence,'
But get out there and score today.

And that's what Ole used to do an awful lot,
He'd come off the bench and score.
When fans saw Ole take off his tracksuit top,
There would be a thunderous roar.

But Ole will always be a Man. United Legend,
And this is the very sure reason,
A Champions League Final last gasp goal, to mend
The Red's all Conquering Treble Season.

So Ole Gunnar Solskjaer you are 'the man,'
Even with the face of a boy.
In front of goal, your nerves were 'dead pan,'
And scoring goals was your favourite ploy.

But he's not left us, he's still working here,
Managing our young reserve team.
Teaching them to shoot on sight, it's clear,
His appointment was right on the 'beam.'

When United couldn't score, but doing all the attacking,
Fergie always had a 'little bit more,'
He'd send on Solskjaer, the 'baby faced assassin.'
And twice he came on and scored four.

Champions League Semi Final.. 2009

Que sera sera,
Whatever will be will be,
We're going to Italy,
Que sera sera.

United verses Arsenal, winners going to Rome,
Champions League Final, United's rightful home.

United win the first leg, a goal by John O,Shea
Who will take the second, is it Arsenal's day?

Second leg starts at Arsenal, fans at top voice,
Quiet after ten minutes, they didn't have a choice.

First Ji Sung Park then Ronaldo, United 2-0 up,
3-0 on aggregate, Arsenal getting whupped.

Beautiful move for third goal, best goal so far,
Arsenal fans start leaving, heading for the car.

Ref then has a brainstorm, Fletcher gets red card,
He now misses the final, life is sometimes hard.

Arsenal score the penalty, aggregate now 4-1,
United still resurgent, Gunners heads have gone.

The eternal city beckons, fans in Trevi Fountain,
Playing Barcelona, now to climb the mountain.

Que sera sera,
Whatever will be will be,
We're going to Italy,
Que sera sera.

Champions League Final --2009

It's the Champions League final, a day out in Rome,
"I've seen the Coliseum, tell me mam at home."
Man United verses Barcelona, winners get it all,
The trophy, the glory, the name for great football.

United start so brightly, Ronaldo wins a free kick,
The ball rebounds to Park, he just can't make the trip.
Gerard Pique gets there first, takes the ball off his toe,
Can't believe the irony, he played for us you know.

Ronaldo's in on everything, he lashed a shot inches wide'
Gets cut down by ugly fouls, as they try to stem the tide.
He fires in a left foot shot and it skims across the goal,
Certainly he's all 'fired up,' but can't 'shovel in the coal.'

But United strangely nervous, now passes going astray,
Can't seem to keep the ball, keep giving it away.
This not the way we planned it, it's not the script we wrote,
Who's playing the football now? Barcelona gets the vote.

Carrick gifts the ball to Iniesta, who slips the ball out wide,
Eto picks it on the run, slips past Vidic, on't inside.
Carrick trying to make amends as Eto pokes the ball
Past Van de Sar to score, and the small man's 'ten feet tall.'

Barca full of confidence now, they pass the ball for fun,
Keep possession for eons, looks like United have not come.
Surely now we'll do something, as we trot out second half,
All our fans believe it as they sing and wave their scarf.

But its not the United we've seen so many times fight back
It seems like a game too far, a game we can not hack.
Its been a great season, we've won so many things,
Yet it's as though we've lost our voice, we just cannot sing.

Lionel Messi scores for Barca a great headed goal,
For them it makes the game secure, a knife into our soul.
Typical of the match for us, our game is way off beam,
Every fan admits, beaten on the night, …by a better team.

Wayne Rooney

At the age of ten Everton first saw the Rooney Boy,
They immediately recognised he was the 'real McCoy.'
Groomed him up through their youth teams,
Aged sixteen he joined the first team scene.
Came on and beat the Arsenal with a 'wonder' goal,
And everybody knew, his was the future, starring role.

For such a star, Everton's stage was not quite big enough,
Though for the Everton fans the decision was tough.
Man United signed him at the age of eighteen,
A more complete footballer Fergie hadn't seen.
He recognised that Rooney was a 'gift from the gods,'
Football gift from the heavens where no 'mere mortal had trod.'

At the age of eighteen he cost twenty seven million pounds,
A snip at the price, the United fans soon found.
Made his debut against Fenerbahce in the Champions League,
Scored a glorious hat-trick that was, in every way, supreme.
The goals were not the result of an opportunist 'sniffer fox,
But each one a great shot from outside the 'box.'

You might think, 'too hard to live up to,' from such a great start,
But Wayne has such a great passion, such a big heart.
Sometimes too great, his temper overflows,
But he wants the right result, and it always shows.
The fans have taken to him, all temper doubts have gone,
A Nobby Stiles, Denis Law, Roy Keane, all 'rolled into one.'

In five short seasons, he's played over two hundred games,
Scored over one hundred goals, to add to his fame.
Won the League Cup, Champion's League and Premiership thrice,
With over fifty caps for England, and twenty five goals, on ice.
He is fulfilling every promise, with a lot to do still .
An effervescent footballer with 'breathtaking skill.'
So just the beginnings of the Rooney Boy's game,
We're expecting a lot more, a lot more of the same.

Michael Owen

There is no doubt that Michael Owen as a goal scorer
at Liverpool was great,
But Fergie has signed him, aged twenty nine, is it all
rather too late?

Has he lost that yard of pace, have bad injuries
taken their toll,
Has he lost his motivation, has he taken his
eye off the ball.

These are the questions that fans are asking, the answers
they all want to invoke.
Is this a massive Fergie gamble, or is it another
of his masterstrokes.

He didn't pull up any trees at Real Madrid and at
Newcastle didn't win any gongs.
I think its fair to say that fans at both clubs are not
singing Michael Owen songs.

But now he's signed for Man United, surely no better
incentive to play well.
It must be true that he'll get better service, and a great
team in which to gel.

In fact I watched him in pre-season score some
tremendous goals.
The link up with Berbatov was encouraging and both
players could further their roles.

I have a feeling the signing is going to be great, another
that's Fergie inspired.
And also he hasn't cost a penny, so it's just like some
One we've hired.

I'd just like to see Michael Owen, score the winning goal
against Liverpool.
It could just happen and again it would show, that
Fergie is no man's fool.

The Greatest Derby Match Ever ?

20th September Two Thousand and Nine,
It's here once again, local derby match time.
New 'big money' City, unbeaten as yet,
Will City's new Tevez hit the back of the net?

The hype is all over, it's now on the pitch,
United fans expecting City's first 'glitch'.
After only two minutes, life is so 'sweet',
Evra's low cross and Rooney's goal is so neat.

But after 16 minutes Ben Foster 's 'in a tizz,'
And gifts the ball to the lurking Tevez,
He passes it back to midfielder Barry,
Find's the empty net, and it's 'cash & carry'.

For the rest of the half, the game 'ebbs and flows',
Till moments before half time, our 'old hero' shows.
Tevez gets the ball in the box, like a City ghost,
But what a crying shame, ...he's gone and hit the post.

United start the 2nd half, like they started the first,
Within a few minutes, a goal scoring burst.
Giggs crosses the ball to the far post,
Fletcher heads it in, and it's 'Sunday Roast'.

But within three minutes, City level once more,
They just won't stop hammering the door.
Bellamy received the ball out on the left flank,
Shoots from 25 yards and it's a 'Sherman Tank'.

This provoked United to some furious attacking,
But Shay Given in goal, not 'given' to slacking.
Two brilliant saves from Berbatov's head,
United not despondent, the games now all 'Red'.

A rising shot from Giggs turned over the top,
Fergie brings on Owen for him to have a 'pop'.
Then Fletcher scores again from a Giggs free kick,
Surely all over now, with only 10 minutes to tick.

But City score again in the last minute of time,
Big mistake from Ferdinand when it all seemed fine.
United fans groan, we've gifted them a draw,
Could be five one but it's ending three all.

Well into stoppage time, six minutes in fact.
Owen is in space, down the left track.
Giggsy gets the ball and pushes it through,
And count on Owen to score a goal for you.

It's there, we've done it, we've won it 4-3,
Better team by far, for all to see.
All down to Owen in the last seconds of time,
Another Fergie triumph when he signed on the line.

We made it difficult, with two daft mistakes,
In spite of their millions, they were no great shakes.
Fergie very nearly at the 'end of his tether',
But could this be 'the greatest derby match ever'?

The Carling Cup Final...2010

The Carling Cup, first trophy of the season,
Let's talk football, not John Terry's treason.
Winning trophies, scoring goals,
Not the girlfriends of Cashley Cole.

It's Aston Villa verses Man United,
The match kicks off, fans all excited.
Within five minutes Vidic brings Agbonlahor down,
Milner converts the pen, and United fans frown.

The midlanders, so early, one nil up,
Claret and Blue cheer, one hand on the cup.
But United's not finished, it's not over yet,
And ten minutes later, they get the ball in the net.

Berbatov robs the poor Richard Dunne,
Ex Man City player, 'oh what fun.'
The ball breaks for Owen, who strokes it in with ease,
For Michael Owen, it's like 'shelling peas.'

But shortly after, Michael Owen 'pulls up.'
A hamstring gone, that's the end of his cup.
But it's the Villa players who silently groan,
Cause Owen goes off, and Rooney comes on.

Man United now, are, 'out of the dark,'
A shot hit's the post from Ji Sung Park.
They now play such attacking football,
But half time comes and it's still one all.

In the second half United look brilliant,
A Carrick save from Friedel shows he is resilient.
But United continue to 'lay on the jam,'
Then substitute Rooney 'breaks through the dam.'

A great cross from Valencia, to Rooney's head,
It loops over Friedel and the cup is now 'red.'
Villa try hard and they do not give up,
But United retain their Carling Cup.

Its United's first trophy of the year,
But still more to fight for, still more to cheer.
There's the Premiership and the Champions League,
If we can win them, only then, we'll be pleased.

The Race for the Premiership 2010

Six games to go and United are one point clear,
Chelsea are close and the end is near.
Unusually Arsenal are still in the race,
Normally, they die and 'sink without trace.'

United 72pts   Chelsea 71   Arsenal 68

This is the big one, Chelsea at ours,
Win this and I'll buy the Misses flowers.
They win 2-1 with a Drogba offside winner,
Linesman allows it like a real beginner.

Five games left, Chelsea now two points in front,
They beat Bolton at home, with a last minute punt.
United only draw at Blackburn with a score of nil-nil,
Arsenal beat Wolves so they're in it still.

Chelsea 77 pts   United 73   Arsenal 71

Chelsea now have a four point lead,
But they lose 2-1 at Spurs, now it's their turn to bleed.
United beat City 1-0 with a winner from Paul Scholes,
Arsenal score twice, then let in three goals.

United now back in it, Chelsea's lead cut to one,
Arsenal are out of it, their hopes truly gone.
Chelsea and United win, Arsenal look on in awe,
Because they can only manage to get a draw.

Chelsea 80 pts   United 79   Arsenal 72

United win at Sunderland but Chelsea won't give in,
With no trouble at all, they get another win.
So it's all down to the final game, another judgement day,
Chelsea still with one point lead, but who will now hold sway.

The final match upon us, but Chelsea hard as nails,
Win 8-0 against Wigan and know they cannot fail.
United beat Stoke 4-0, yet the 'Prem' is 'beyond the wire,'
United fans choke tears and can only begrudgingly admire.

Final Table.....Chelsea 86 pts United 85 Arsenal 75

**One thing is clear, Sir Alex won't get the 'sack,
One thing is certain, Man United will be back.**

Not
The End

Just waiting for more.

Be sure to look out for Man United Poetry in motion..
        ...Book Two.

Will Include....
Poems about others of United's great games and players.

Final of Cup Winners Cup verses Barcelona.
Final of Champions League verses Bayern Munich.

Roger Byrne
Duncan Edwards
Tommy Taylor
Paddy Crerand
Mark Hughes
Denis Irwin
Steve Bruce
Gary Pallister
Alex Stepney
David May
Gary Neville
Roy Keane
Nobby Stiles
Edwin Van der Sar
Gordon McQueen
Ruud Van Nystleroy
Dimitar Berbatov
The Neville brothers
Nemanya Vidic

Also 'hopefully' poems about great games yet to be played,
And great stars yet to be made.

For more books or more Man United...Poetry in Motion
memorabilia go online to:- www.mupoetryinmotion.co.uk

CPSIA information can be obtained
at www.ICGtesting.com
Printed in the USA
2400LVUK00005B

9 781456 784225